Love Human
and Divine

Love Human
and Divine

REFLECTIONS ON
Love, Sexuality, and Friendship

L. William Countryman

morehouse

HARRISBURG • LONDON

Morehouse Publishing, P.O. Box 1321, Harrisburg, PA 17105
Morehouse Publishing, The Tower Building, 11 York Road, London SE1 7NX
Morehouse Publishing is a Continuum imprint.

Cover design by Corey Kent

Library of Congress Cataloging-in-Publication Data

A catalog record of this book is available from the Library of Congress.

Printed in the United States of America

05 06 07 08 09   10 9 8 7 6 5 4 3 2 1

For Tom Schultz OHC,
with thanks for years of conversation
and counsel

CONTENTS

THE
REASONS
FOR THIS
BOOK

$\mathcal{P}$ASSION, TODAY, IS A GREAT—INDEED, A PASSION-
ate—topic. The eros that is a fundamental part of
human existence seems to some to be undermin-
ing the institutions so painstakingly built over
millennia to contain it. For these people, it threat-
ens to flood out and swamp civilized society. For
others, the present seems rather a time of recognizing age-old hypocrisies and righting millen-
nial injustices. For them, it is the moment to
rebuild in more just and more authentically
human ways. Either way, eros is at the center of
much of our public conflict.

At the same time, vast numbers of people
experience eros as a central element in their lives,
an element that gives them meaning, form, and
direction. It is critical to the bond established in
marriage. It is an integral part of adult human
existence, whether expressed in sexual relationships or in other kinds of passionate relationships

with the world and the people around us. It imparts life and color to a world that would be rather gray, were it composed entirely of duty and logic. I shall argue here that one of its qualities is to give us insight into our relationship with God and God's relationship with us. Clearly, eros is immensely powerful, whether for good or ill.

The Christian churches are at a critical point in dealing with eros and its place in the life of faith and spirituality. Western culture, after being deeply suspicious of sex and eros for almost two millennia, has begun to realize that it is an inescapable—and inescapably important—element of humanity. Indeed, it is the source of much of our human energy—energy that can be turned to the service of creation or of destruction. Other cultures have dealt with sexuality and eros somewhat differently from that of the West. But, given the pervasiveness of Western culture in the world today, no other culture is entirely immune to its effects, either to the eros-negative tradition it long fostered or to the questioning and revision of that tradition that is now going on. Christians in both Western and non-Western contexts must deal with these issues in ways that, while not identical, nonetheless manifest many of the same conflicts. For the eros-negative quality of Western culture has long found its particular home in the Christian religion.

The conflicts in the churches and in society as a whole have emerged primarily in three areas: gender, sexual orientation, and sexual violence. In the area of gender, people have come to question long-standing assumptions that reserved roles of public prominence to men. Women now figure as heads of state and government, as ordained leaders in religious communities, as leaders of business, and as major figures in the arts. The struggle over this development, however, is far from being over. For every country that has a woman as head of government, there is at least one where women are routinely repressed and prevented from acting as full citizens. In the religious sphere, some Christian traditions remain emphatically opposed to including women in ordained leadership and others are threatened with division over the topic.

Even within denominations that ordain women, those opposed to it often create coalitions, formal or informal, to exclude them.

People have also begun to take more seriously the realities of sexual abuse. Once we tended to see rape or the sexual abuse of children as individual, isolated acts—and, too often, to assume that the victim must have enticed the aggressor. Increasingly, we recognize that these acts may function as perverse and violent ways of reinforcing deeply embedded social hierarchies: the dominance of men over women and of the stronger (adults) over the weaker (children). Indeed, we have seen rape used as an instrument of policy in wars, alongside episodes of "ethnic cleansing" or out-and-out genocide. In the church itself, the failure of authorities to take adequate precautions to prevent the abuse of children by clergy seems to arise from a sense that the church's own facade of innocence is more important than its duty to defend the weak. Here, too, the conflict is far from over. The international community has been slow to protect the well-being of women in contexts of social violence. And some churches have been painfully slow, clumsy, and even, at times, cynical in coming to terms with their own responsibilities in cases where their clergy or other representatives have abused children in their charge.

The single most volatile area in which the issue of eros has come to the fore is that of sexual orientation. Many people have begun to ask whether same-gender sexual orientation is really the alarming perversion that we of the West long considered it. Can it, in fact, provide as much opportunity as opposite-gender sexual orientation for forms of human bonding that are creative and constructive? Here, the question of eros comes directly to the fore. It is a question of what eros is, what roles it may have to play in human society and in our relation to God, how we can understand it as an integral part of who we are and not merely as a source of temptation, an occasion of sin, and a prelude to punishment. The idea of including the committed partnerships of lesbians and gay men within the institution of marriage is proving particularly controversial, in both the ecclesiastical and the political

spheres. Its opponents raise the threat that it will
create major rents in our social fabric—and sometimes threaten to create such rents themselves by
tearing apart churches if they should allow it. Con-
servative Christians have thrown large amounts of
money into preventing political change. The same
intense emotions greet the move toward ordaining
openly gay and lesbian clergy, for this, too, is a
sacramental recognition of the possibility for same-
gender eros to convey God's blessings.

These are the issues that have prompted the
writing of this little book. But you will not find
much here that is directly focused on them. This
is because I believe that they are, in large part, the
consequences of a deeper problem and cannot be
dealt with without first stepping further back to
deal with that problem. Eros is a dangerous thing,
full of power. We can easily feel threatened by it.
But we cannot make it safe merely by confining
it, much less by repressing it. If we have learned
nothing else from Dr. Freud and the host of modern students of sex, we should have learned this.
The question, then, is how to deal with eros in

creative rather than destructive ways. To do so, we must bring it into the center of our spirituality—our encounter with God and the way of life that flows out of that encounter. It belongs in the center of all our thinking about good and evil, about what gives true meaning to our existence, about our common humanity and the ways in which we succeed in living it out—or fail to do so.

These concerns, of course, are not limited to Christians. But we who are Christians must contemplate them in the context of our faith. Where does eros belong in our particular understanding of God, rooted as it is in the good news of Jesus? We have often shied away from this question. From the second century onward, Christians were convinced that celibacy (or, better yet, virginity) was superior to any actively lived-out sexuality. If human sexuality was to be expressed in action at all, it must be tightly limited and controlled. Even when we have taken up the question of eros, there has often been at least a tacit assumption that we must suppress any earthly love if we wish to participate in the true love of God. My goal in this little meditation is to reject that tendency and to put love—passionate, erotic love—back in the central place that it deserves in our Christian spirituality. My point is not to explain in detail how this will work. We do not yet know in any full, rich detail how it will work. My point, rather, is to insist that we must learn—and must engage faithfully, deliberately, and actively in this learning.

If the churches can learn this, Western culture can learn it along with us. If Western culture can learn this, the churches need to be part of the process. Otherwise, we are in danger of having two parallel cultures, one religious and one secular, and neither of them will have anything truly holy or profound to say about the central human experience of erotic attraction, connection, and fulfillment. And yet, the erotic *is* holy. Whether it takes the form of a sexual relationship or of other intimate connections, we find here our most common experience of transcendence—the experience that allows us to recognize the Holy when we encounter it and to speak of it to one another, even though it always seems to be beyond words.[1]

LOVE
HUMAN
AND
DIVINE

CHRISTIANS HAVE A LONG AND COMPLICATED relationship with love, sexuality, and friendship. Jesus chose two commandments about love as the great commandments that sum up the whole Law, thus putting love—the love of God and the love of our neighbor—at the very heart of our religious life (Mark 12:28–34). As if that were not enough, the Johannine literature in the New Testament, particularly the Gospel and the First Letter of John, return repeatedly to the issue of love: "This is my commandment, that you love one another as I have loved you" (John 15:12). "Whoever does not love does not know God, for God is love" (1 John 4:8). "Those who do not love a brother or sister whom they have seen, cannot love God whom they have not seen" (1 John 4:20). Paul, too, strikes the same note: "Love does no wrong to a neighbor; therefore, love is the fulfilling of the law" (Rom 13:10).

Love is clearly central to Christian spirituality. But does that include something as specific and limited as friendship? Something as physical as sexual attraction? Modern English, like ancient Hebrew, has essentially a single word for love. But ancient Greek had several; and even Latin's rather limited vocabulary provided two.[2] Some Christian thinkers have used the multiplicity of Greek terms as an opportunity to define several different and even mutually exclusive types of love. *Agape*, the holy love, it is claimed, has nothing to do with *eros*, the love of another human being.[3]

Others (I count myself among them) think this multiplication of loves overinterprets the linguistic differences. Certainly, we also have to recognize that human beings sometimes use and enjoy our loves well and sometimes not. Love is subject to as many temptations and has as many chances to go wrong as any other aspect of human existence, even religion. Like religion, it is not always a good thing in practice, however good it seems in theory. Whether it is singular or plural, then, love is complex and challenging. Indeed, sometimes the love

14

that claims to be purest turns out to be the most destructive and evil, for we do not always understand our own loves or present them honestly.

To complicate things further, the scriptures sometimes speak of love in dualistic terms. "Do not love the world or the things in the world. The love of the Father is not in those who love the world" (1 John 2:15). The impulse to oppose this-worldly love to other-worldly love—the love of people, places, and things to the love of God alone—has been powerful in our spiritual traditions. When one balances it all out, it sometimes seems less than clear whether Christianity is in favor of love at all, at least in the ordinary sense of the word.

At the same time, there have been voices within the tradition that sing a very different tune. I want to follow up on two of them here and see what sort of alternative perspective they can offer us. I organize my thoughts here in the form of some commentary and reflections on four texts, one scriptural, the other three from a writer in my own Anglican tradition.

I

The Rose of Sharon

I am the rose of Sharon, and the lily
   of the valleys.
As the lily among thorns, so is my love
   among the daughters.
As the apple tree among the trees of the wood,
   so is my beloved among the sons.
I sat down under his shadow with
   great delight, and his fruit was sweet
   to my taste.
He brought me to the banqueting house,
   and his banner over me was love.
Stay me with flagons, comfort me with apples:
   for I am sick of love.
His left hand is under my head, and his right
   hand doth embrace me.

—SONG OF SOLOMON 2:1–6 (AV)

WHAT IS THE SONG OF SONGS (OR SONG OF Solomon, as it is also called) doing in the middle of the Christian scriptures? Christians have, I think, been a little embarrassed by its presence. We distance its overt sexuality by insisting that it is an allegory of the love of God for the church or for the individual soul. Christian liturgy has largely ignored it and seldom assigns it to be read at public worship.[4] Too much heavy breathing! Even in the King James Version, which I just quoted, it's a very erotic poem; and that becomes still clearer in good modern translations like those by Marcia Falk or by Ariel Bloch and Chana Bloch.[5] It seems an odd, almost alien, object in the universe of Biblical documents, and scholars have labored long and hard to discern its origins and explain its inclusion in the canon.

If we turn, however, to the history of private reading of the Song of Songs among Christians, we find a different story. It was one of the first Biblical books to receive a full commentary—from no less a figure than Origen, a third-century theologian and scholar who was the first truly great Christian thinker after Paul and John. In the Middle Ages, it received many commentaries from both Jews and Christians.[6] Most Christians may not have read it in public after the Reformation, but even Puritans wrote commentaries on it. And if you don't know Song of Solomon pretty well, you will miss much of the nuance of seventeenth-century English religious poetry. It was critically important to Roman Catholic traditions of spirituality, too; John of the Cross, for example, would be unintelligible without it.

In the Rabbinic order of the Scriptures of Israel, the Song belongs to the Writings, the least authoritative division of scripture. One could argue that this makes it a relatively marginal work. For Christians, however, it is more difficult to make that case. The book falls right in the middle of our canon and belongs to the same part of scripture as the Psalms, of which we have made heavy use, both public and private. Though it is not cited in the New Testament, it is echoed and alluded to.[7]

This pattern of attention to or neglect of the Song reflects our ambivalence about eros itself. (The word for "love," incidentally, in the Old Greek translation of Song of Songs—the version used by most early Christians—is *agape*, not *eros*; but it is quite clear that the text is speaking the language of erotic, sexual love.) If the Song seems marginal to us today, that is a by-product of our history of reading. It's not at all inevitable. Try taking it, instead, as central.[8] Beginning there, what else might you see in scripture? For one thing, you might notice that the Bible begins with sex, which is the one feature of human existence that both creation narratives specifically mention. (Genesis 1 speaks of it in terms of procreation, Genesis 2 in terms of companionship. But they agree that it is intrinsic to our divinely created humanity.) You might also notice that the Bible ends sexually, with the marriage supper of the Lamb (Rev 21).

And in between, you will notice that eros is a topic of repeated concern, sometimes because it is an occasion of abuse, sometimes in order to restrain it and give it a place in the social order, sometimes to rejoice in its procreative potential, sometimes to reassert its power to bond us to one another, sometimes to celebrate God's passionate love for Israel or the church. And here, in the Song itself, eros is celebrated because it is beautiful and revelatory and compelling. This little collection of love poetry, based in ancient Near Eastern traditions,[9] is striking in the way the two lovers treat one another as equals, in the openness and vulnerability of the passion they express, in the risks they take to further their relationship, in the way the erotic bond is sufficient by itself, without the trappings of marriage and social status, to explain their connection. They are far indeed from the patriarchal model of the ancient household, focused as it was on differences in power: one man's power as husband over wife, as father over children, as master over slaves and clients and hired hands and assorted hangers-on.

We can, of course, read Song of Solomon allegorically in reference to the love of God. Hosea and Ephesians both use human erotic love for just this purpose. But there is nothing in the text itself that limits us to allegory. It reads perfectly well in its simplest and most direct sense, as a dialogue of lovers. This does not therefore make the allegorical reading wrong. But it reminds us that even our allegorical reading is dependent for its power on the ordinary human experience of eros. If we cannot let Song of Songs speak of literal human love, it will lose its power to speak to us of the love of God.

Here the Song's real importance to the Holy Scriptures and to Christian faith begins to become apparent. From first to last, the Bible portrays God as passionate. This portrayal collides with the later theological dictum that God is "without body, parts, or passions." I do not suggest that either the Bible or later theology is wrong. They are making different points about God, using different metaphorical points of reference. All talk about God is metaphorical. The problem is that we sometimes forget that this is as true of metaphysical-sounding statements as of any other. As a result, the metaphors of abstract theology have often sounded to us like simple, literal descriptions of God, and they have dominated our discourse to the point of excluding the emotive metaphors more characteristic of scripture.

Christianity grew shy of the emotive metaphors in part because it "came of age" and took on classic form in the Mediterranean world of the Late Roman Empire (third to sixth centuries). This was a culture increasingly concerned about human vulnerability and increasingly suspicious of the role that eros and other passions play in creating this vulnerability. There were many elements at work in this complex process. The early Christian turn toward virginity (a topic rare in scripture itself) had its roots in the Stoic ideal of *apatheia*, of freedom from passion. This heritage combined with a spirituality that increasingly saw the development of the individual's relationship with God as incompatible with familial and social responsibilities; hermits like Antony of Egypt "fled" into the desert to escape them. And the resulting practice of virginity spread partly because of the relative freedom that it opened up for women, who now, almost for the first time, had an opportunity to lead lives defined by their own purposes rather than the will of their father or husband.[10]

Augustine of Hippo provides us with a convenient illustration of some of the basic characteristics of this turn away from eros. His one long-term sexual relationship was with a concubine, not a full wife. It seems to have offered him little in relational terms (no Song of Songs here!). After his conversion, he dismissed his concubine. We never even learn her name. In later theologizing, he used the penis as an emblem of the fallen human predicament; the fact that a man's erections are not under voluntary control signified for him that the body is in revolt against the mind and will. The Fall created chaos within us, and the erotic element in our human makeup—particularly the male makeup—virtually defines the rebel camp.[11]

Christianity has historically been stretched between an affirmation of sexuality, so that it can serve its allegorical function, and a deep fear that it is at the very heart of human alienation from God. It is not surprising, of course, that any cultural or religious tradition would be of two minds about the erotic. You don't need very broad experience of human life to know that eros can have both constructive and destructive expressions. It is not simply the fact of Christian ambivalence that is worth noting, but the depth of it and the Christian tendency to metaphysicalize it, to think of certain dimensions of the erotic (those addressed to other people) as evil and others (those directed to God) as alone good.

Yet, the presence of the Song of Solomon in our scriptures has meant that we could never go all the way down this dualistic path. There have always been other possibilities within our tradition. I turn now to my second quotation, taken from meditations written by Thomas Traherne, a late-seventeenth-century poet and priest in the Church of England. Traherne specifically rejects the notion that love for God is intrinsically and inevitably opposed to love for the created order. He makes this point in a variety of ways, most of them not at all sexual. And this makes him a particularly good starting point for constructing a more positive theological discourse about eros, variously realized as love, sexuality, and friendship.

II

God Alone—
Cannot Be
Beloved

There is in love two strange perfections, that make it infinite in Goodness. It is infinitely diligent in doing good, and it infinitely delighteth in that Goodness. It taketh no pleasure comparable in anything to that it taketh in exalting and blessing. And therefore hath it made thee a comprehension infinite to see all ages, and an affection endless to love all Kingdoms, and a power fathomless to enjoy all Angels. And a thirst unsatiable to desire and delight in them. And a never-wearied faculty all-sufficient to love, number, take in, prize, and esteem all the varieties of creatures and their excellencies in all Worlds, that thou mayest enjoy them in communion with Him. It is all obligation that He requires it. What

life wouldst thou lead? Wouldst thou love
God alone? God alone cannot be beloved. He
cannot be loved with a finite love, because
He is infinite. Were He beloved alone, His love
would be limited. He must be loved in all with
an illimited love, even in all His doings, in all
His friends, in all His creatures. Everywhere
in all things thou must meet His love. And
this the Law of Nature commands. And it is
thy glory that thou art fitted for it. His love
unto thee is the law and measure of thine unto
Him: His love unto all others the law and
obligation of thine unto all.

—THOMAS TRAHERNE, *CENTURIES*, 1.72[12]

"WOULDST THOU LOVE GOD ALONE? GOD ALONE cannot be beloved." The statement seems shocking at first. It takes a moment to realize that it is really a paraphrase of the Summary of the Law. It restates the claim of 1 John that if you don't love your brother or sister whom you have seen, you can't love God whom you've not seen. And yet, there is something more going on here. One could conceivably read 1 John as if it were speaking about love purely as a kind of duty. If you are not trying to be helpful and caring toward the people with whom you share the community of faith, you cannot be said to love God. Traherne's ecstatic style makes it pretty clear that he is not just talking about duty. He's talking about passion.

There is certainly an element of ethics here, too: "His love unto thee is the law and measure of thine unto Him: His love unto all others the law

and obligation of thine unto all." But ethics is not
the starting point for Traherne; it is consequence.
It is the consequence of awe, wonder, delight,
love—the consequence of passion. God's passion
for us and for the whole of creation is what sum-
mons us to a comparable passion. And that passion must necessarily work itself out in our
behavior with and toward the beloved. I say
"work itself out." It is not enough to say "express
itself," as if one could know love in advance and
merely needed to put it into action. Life with the
beloved is not merely a consequence of love, but
the context in which love discovers itself, grows,
matures, is refined and enlarged.

The eros that attaches us to God and the eros
that attaches us to the world around us and to specific human beings are not in competition with
one another. Both flow from God's passionate love
for us and for the creation of which we are a part.
This return to the notion of a Creator passionately
engaged with the creation is a key necessity for us
here and now in the history of Christianity. This
is most obviously true in the realm of ecology, as

we face the sweeping damage we have already done to the world around us and the threat of significant disruptions yet to come. We are compelled to confront the truth that we have dishonored the Artist's work even as we claimed to love and worship the Artist. But the failures are equally grave in the realm of our human relationships.

All significant human relationships are in some sense manifestations of the power of eros. They manifest themselves very differently depending on their context, but all flow from the power we have to be attracted by one another, to take delight in one another, to find delight opening us to a new kind of communion with one another. In this respect, friendship is as much the work of eros as is sexual partnership, not because it implies sexual attraction (sometimes it even seems to exclude it) but because it is founded on desire to draw close to my friend and on the delight I take in my friend's presence.

This drive toward *connection* is fundamental to our humanity. The specifically sexual forms of eros are an important subcategory of it, not the whole. We tend to assume that the story of God's forming Eve from Adam's side is about the creation of sexual companionship. But in the twelfth century, Aelred of Rievaulx read it as being about the creation of friendship and of community. In fact, he treated it as the origin of monastic community.[13] Our tendency to separate sexual eros absolutely from the broader eros that generates such connections seems to me misplaced.

Traherne is talking in very broad terms about the passionate power of connection. It can bring us into communion not only with God and with one another, but with every element in creation, from rocks to seraphim. Whether your connection with rocks takes the form of a collector's enthusiasm, a scientific delight in geology, an experience of mysticism in the natural world, or a sculptor's intimacy with marble is secondary. Whether your relatedness with another human takes the form of a lifelong nonsexual friendship or a lifelong sexual partnership, shared membership on a team or mutual esteem in the workplace, a sibling relationship or the bond of teacher and student, they all proceed from the same erotic power of relating.

This does not mean that all these forms are interchangeable or that they can substitute for one another. They are not. There are good reasons related to our personal integrity—"integrity" both in the sense of "moral responsibility" and in the sense of "personal wholeness"—why they are not. Teachers, for example, know that there is an erotic power in the process of teaching and learning; and we know that it is best left there as a kind of ionic charge that may help bring down the lightning of discovery. To literalize it into an affair with a student is normally if not always to reduce its educational power.

Yet, all expressions of love are interrelated. Friendship is a passionate connection that does not require sexual expression. On the other hand, a rich and enduring sexual partnership probably does require friendship as an element in it.[14] We shortchange the sexual expression of eros if we think of it simply as the satisfaction of physical desire. It is much more than that. The desire is rooted as much in the soul and spirit as in the body. And it is supremely satisfied when it enables a genuinely transcendent union with the beloved, a union that belongs as much to soul and spirit as to body.

And the human capacity to love—the capacity that grounds both the possibility of union with God and the possibility of union with another human being—this capacity is not multiple. There is not one love directed toward God and another toward the beloved. In the same way, the love directed toward God and the love directed toward the beloved do not mean that our capacity to love is divided. As Traherne writes, God "must be loved in all with an illimited love, even in all His doings, in all His friends, in all His creatures."

And yet, in one respect, I may seem to be moving in exactly the opposite direction from my text. Traherne is saying "in all." I am saying, "Yes, and perhaps also in this particular one." Not only is there a love poured out on creation at large; there is a love directed at this particular friend, at this other who is my beloved. I do, in fact, have a quar-

rel with one element in Traherne's text—an element appropriate enough to the kind of meditation he was writing, but easy to take in a way that
winds up being destructive of human faithfulness.

In the *Centuries* of meditations, from which I
have drawn this text, Traherne repeatedly cele-
brates the human capacity to enjoy and celebrate
in a nonpossessive way, a capacity he first discov-
ered in himself in childhood.[15] It is a capacity that
can rescue us from narrow defensiveness and
grasping jealousy and open the path to a more
generous kind of existence. When he speaks of it,
however, as "illimited," as "infinite," he plays into a
favorite Christian temptation: the temptation to
abandon the finite world for illusions of infinity.

Theology tends to focus on infinity, not only
the infinity of God but that of universal principles. However understandable and even necessary
in some ways, this is potentially escapist. Finitude
is the reality of humanity, the water in which, like
fish, we swim. At first, we hardly notice it. But then
we become aware of it as an affront: the failing
body, the lapsing memory, the distance we cannot

traverse, the result we cannot achieve, the years we cannot live. It is important, as corrective, to recognize that the finite is also gift. One basic form in which this comes to us is the experience of beauty, another the experience of sexual transcendence.

Consider the experience of beauty. I sat, one morning in the early spring, looking out through the window at a pot of freesias. Their green, swordlike foliage was brilliantly lit by the early sun, as were their flowers, starting at the base a pale yellow and brightening quickly to an intense, almost pure red. Behind them, a few hundred feet away, was a house clad with shingles, weathered dark by years of winter rains and now shaded from the low sun by nearby trees. The only object close to the freesias was a four-by-four timber, painted white, serving as a porch-post. The angle of the sun made one of the sides seem brilliantly white, the other the particular shade of gray that conveys "shadow on white paint."

The beauty of the leaves and flowers was dependent on their form, their limitations, their finitude. There was an economical grace in their shapes that reminded me of ballet or modern dance, where forms very like these reappear in motion and gesture.

The colors were also a gift of finitude. Red is not green is not yellow. And thereby each became capable of carrying its own layers of significance. The red of the flowers suggested light and warmth and a spring that, on this early March day, was not yet quite present with us. The green suggested a rootedness—in this case, in a terra cotta pot hidden by the windowsill—promising continuity and renewal, even when the freesias die back and return to their resting state.

The impression made by the flowers was heightened by the position of the sun. It would never again be quite the same that day, though they would remain beautiful. Not only the illumination falling on them, but the shadow on the house beyond, transformed them. They were, from the place where I sat, almost isolated in space, like a sculpture at the center of a large and otherwise empty gallery. They were a source of delight. And it all came as the gift of finitude.

The magic of our sexual attractions and the enduring partnerships founded on them is not radically different. It is the specificity of *this* beloved human being that is so powerful: this person's beauty and grace and light—a beauty and grace and light fully visible only to the lover's eyes. Love is the longing for conjunction with the beloved, the delight of that conjunction, the delight of uniting two finite beings, the joy of working out a life together.

In their union, the lovers become more than each one is individually. Only in our finitude can we appreciate the beauty of the other, the delight of the approach; and yet, even as we remain our separate selves, the union of lovers provides the movement into transcendence, whereby we may become more than simply our separate selves. This transcendence is not limited to sexual union, though it may be most powerful and indisputable there. It is a characteristic of solid friendships, too, manifest in the ability of old friends to sit together in companionable silence. But whatever form transcendence takes, it is rooted in the fulfillment of desire, made possible by eros working in the context of our finitude.

We are finite beings, and we must love finitely. God is infinite and must be loved in an "illimited" way. How do we reconcile these opposites? We love finitely, but in a way that is open to the infinity of God's love. Our love of the stone is also, without denying its own integrity, a way of loving God; our love of the human beloved is also, without denying its own integrity, a way of loving God. What is more, every genuine love promotes every other genuine love. The proverbial self-absorption of lovers is only a stage. If their love matures, it will become not only a delight to them but a sign of love to others, a hearth at which others warm themselves. It will become not something for them to contemplate and enjoy for themselves alone, but a reminder that love is the greatest gift we have to offer others as well.

Love Is
a Phoenix

Since Love will thrust in itself as the greatest
of all principles, let us at last willingly allow
it room. I was once a stranger to it, now I
am familiar with it as a daily acquaintance.
'Tis the only heir and benefactor of the world.
It seems it will break in everywhere, as that
without which the world could not be enjoyed.
Nay as that without which it would not be
worthy to be enjoyed. For it was beautified
by love, and commandeth the love of a Donor
to us. Love is a Phoenix that will revive in its
own ashes, inherit death, and smell sweetly
in the grave.

—THOMAS TRAHERNE, *Centuries,* 4.61[16]

*E*ROS IS IMPORTANT TO CHRISTIANS BECAUSE IT touches on the love that is at the very heart of our faith, of our relationship with God. But is this passionate love really what the author of 1 John meant in writing that "God is love"? Surely, we think, the love that God *is* can't be erotic love; it must be something higher, cleaner, purer than that.

Christians have long endeavored to think of our faith and our vocation as centered in such a higher, purer love. We contrast it with eros by saying that eros wants to possess the object of love whereas agape wants only to give. Agape is the love that seeks nothing in return, that wishes only to benefit the one loved. It is the love that God exemplifies for us in the great act of creation, in the unearned grace with which God seeks out the lost sheep, in the generosity of the Age to Come.

No, I don't think so. I'm not sure that that's even an accurate description of God's love, and I am certain it is not a good model for human beings. Even God, if we trust the scriptures, wants something of us, wants love in return. God created even the great whales for the sake of delight—theirs as well as God's (Ps. 104:26). God created us and gave us freedom so that, through us, the creation might share in the sublime exchange of love within the Trinity itself. God wants our love, invites our love—but never compels our love. If we take the metaphors of scripture seriously, we shall have to say that God's love is erotic and that our own erotic love is a key metaphor for recognizing and speaking of God's.

Our hankering after an utterly selfless love, by contrast, does not seem to me to have good effects on human beings. I have seen it at work in the lives of seminarians and clergy and finally come to the conclusion that it is something to be warned against. Even if such a love is conceivable in God, it is not in human beings. We are finite, not infinite. We have to be fed if we are to feed others. We rightly long for our love to be returned because that is how human beings transcend our individual isolation and come into communion with one another. This does not mean that we never give simply and without thought of return. Nor does it mean that we grasp at the love of others; indeed, such grasping destroys the very possibility of genuine love. But it does mean that we are not made to live forever in the state of pure, unrequited giving.

Erotic love is not inherently grasping and selfish. That is the misuse, the abuse of eros, not its intrinsic nature. But it does desire a return of love because that is what it exists to bring about, the very function it subserves whether in the life of the Holy Trinity or in our lives as part of God's creation. We Christians would do well to acknowledge this need rather than trying to "rise above it" and be without desires, without needs.

It's a truism that Christianity is focused on love—and equally a truism that we fail to live up to that. I attribute this at least partly to excessive and unreal notions of the nature of the love to which we are called. If we try to exhibit a bottomless love, we quickly run dry and grow angry. Our attitudes toward those with whom we disagree decay easily into a savage hostility. The eros that informs our human loves—including our sexual loves—is a better model. It is, indeed, an integral part of what draws us into relationship with God. And our experience of this eros teaches us what love is, what it feels like, what it means to give it and to receive it. And it teaches us *what it is not.*[17]

To know a love that is achieving its goal of communion is to know both ourselves and God anew. The inquisitor who burns you at the stake for your own good, the moralist who represses your gifts and your loves out of what he pretends to be love for you—both these and their victims are casualties of our warfare against our own finitude and against the eros by which we transcend it. They care only for universal principles; they know nothing of real human connection. If they could say of love, with Traherne, "I was once a stranger to it, now I am familiar with it as a daily acquaintance," they would abandon their careers with tears of repentance. As it stands, they make a hell all around themselves.

The Song of Songs enshrines this love in the heart of our scriptures: the love of the human beloved is our closest, most decisive analogy to the love of God. Both loves are difficult to express adequately. But somehow poets, from antiquity to today, have learned how to write of this skittish, well-camouflaged beast we call "eros." You may not think that love poetry is important to Christian faith, but if the poetry of human love ever ceased to exist, we would lose the best means we have to speak of our drawing near to God.

Gay men and lesbians often have a circuitous process of learning this. At some point in life we have to discover that the largely heterosexual poetry of love that we encountered in school is actually speaking of the same eros that inhabits our souls, even if it doesn't always get the pronouns right. (And, of course, there is far more lesbian and gay love poetry than we were allowed to know about a few decades back.) In this way, we discover that the poetry of love, no matter what the orientation of the poet, belongs to all human beings because it deals with something absolutely basic to our humanity.

And it can become, for us as Christians, a doorway to God. Let me be clear again what I am saying here. I don't mean that human eros is always beautiful or innocent. For that matter, our human love of God, concretized in religion, is not always beautiful or innocent. History tells us that either can become mixed up with greed, with hatred, with violence.

What I am saying is that, without human eros, we would have almost no analogy for our relationship with God. Flawed as all human eros is, it is still the best thing in our makeup, the brightest treasure that God placed there. And it is by this that God calls us home.

For love has a power to triumph even over our own abuse of it. It keeps coming back. It keeps sneaking up on us. It keeps breaking us open and showing us new worlds outside the thick carapaces we have formed around ourselves. It shows us one another and it shows us God. "Love," says Traherne, "is a Phoenix that will revive in its own ashes, inherit death, and smell sweetly in the grave."

Joys Down
from Heaven…

LOVE

  O nectar! O delicious stream!
O ravishing and only pleasure! Where
   Shall such another theme
Inspire my tongue with joys,
  or please mine ear!
   Abridgement of delights!
    And queen of sights!
O mine of rarities! O kingdom wide!
O more! O cause of all! O glorious bride!
  O God! O bride of God! O king!
  O soul and crown of everything!

Did not I covet to behold
Some endless monarch, that did always live
    In palaces of gold,
Willing all kingdoms, realms,
   and crowns to give
     Unto my soul! Whose love
      A spring might prove
Of endless glories, honours, friendships,
   pleasures,
Joys, praises, beauties, and celestial treasures!
    Lo, now I see there's such a King,
    The fountainhead of everything!

Did my ambition ever dream
Of such a Lord, of such a love! Did I
    Expect so sweet a stream
As this at any time! Could any eye
    Believe it? Why, all power
     Is used here

Joys down from Heaven on my head
    to shower,
And Jove beyond the fiction doth appear
    Once more in golden rain to come
    To Danae's pleasing, fruitful womb.

    His Ganymede! His life! His joy!
Or He comes down to me, or takes me up
    That I might be His boy,
And fill, and taste, and give,
    and drink the cup.
    But these (tho great) are all
      Too short and small,
Too weak and feeble pictures to express
The true mysterious depths of blessedness.
    I am His image, and His friend.
    His son, bride, glory, temple, end.[18]

               —THOMAS TRAHERNE

*T*HIS PASSIONATE POEM ASTONISHES IN MORE
than one way. One is the freedom with which Traherne mingles biblical images with those drawn
from classical antiquity—perhaps a little less
astonishing in the late seventeenth century than it
is today. Another is the way it brings heterosexual
and homosexual (and for that matter sexual and
nonsexual) metaphors together to describe our
relationship with God. Whether the speaker is
being Danae, receiving Zeus in a shower of gold,
or Ganymede snatched up to Olympus, he is rev-
eling in intimacy with the Holy. (For some, the
image of Ganymede may sound more like ped-
erasty than an adult same-sex union. I feel uncom-
fortable with it for that reason myself. One does
have to remember, however, that in the seventeenth century as in classical antiquity, sexual relationships of whatever kind often involved a fairly
substantial age difference.)

What is particularly significant about the poem is the experience of *delight* it embodies and conveys. This is not dutiful religion. This is a religion based on intimacy, an intimacy that requires a great variety of images to try to express it:

> But these (tho great) are all
>   Too short and small,
> Too weak and feeble pictures to express
> The true mysterious depths of blessedness.
>   I am His image, and His friend.
>   His son, bride, glory, temple, end.

The eros that informs and animates this vision is not narrowly heterosexual or homosexual. It is not exclusively sexual at all. "Friend" here turns out to be as powerful an image as "son" or "bride." But it is definitely erotic in its passionate celebration of communion and transcendence. And it is this erotic quality of our relationship with God that presents the great challenge to the church of our time and forms the common thread in the many questions we face about gender and sexuality.

I am particularly conscious of this in the conflict over the status of lesbian and gay members of the church. We have always been here. The great difference today is that we are here visibly and openly, that we do not quietly retire to our closets anymore, and that our presence now has to be noticed. Either we must be driven out, or the Christian communities of faith will have to come to terms with our presence, which, of course, means coming to terms with whatever God is up to in drawing us here.

We are not, of course, here because it's such a nice place for us. Mostly it is not, though increasingly there are also some genuinely welcoming manifestations of the church. We're not here just to make trouble, either. Some of us may enjoy that, at least for a year or two; some of us don't like it at all. I'm one of those. But we have a strong enough sense of calling and relationship to God—a strong enough sense that God wants us here—that we stay put anyway. Why is God doing this? I think it is to give others a chance to be saved.

Sometimes, well-meaning liberal heterosexuals say, "Couldn't you people just hang back a little and not endanger the church by asking for so much so soon?" To that, my answer is, "The issue of gay/lesbian presence in the church may be the most important thing the church has to deal with in our time, because it is really the issue of whether Christians can reclaim God's gift of eros."

I do not mean to slight the other very real sufferings of the world—the disaster, say, of AIDS in Africa or the unfinished struggle against racism throughout the world or the chaos threatened by religious fundamentalisms. These require our concern and our work. We have yet fully to grasp their magnitude or the extent of our complicity in them. At the same time, these are evils of a more familiar kind. We at least know where to begin in responding to them.

Our suspicion of eros is an older and a deeper flaw—and one deeply implicated, I think, in our own Christian history of cruelty and abuse toward one another and the rest of the world.[19]

No one can say exactly why God has called so many gay men and lesbians into the church or why God has prompted us to make our presence a public fact. But I think it is, above all, in the hope that our presence will awaken the church to the significance of eros for all Christian faith and life—not because we are any more erotic than heterosexual people, but because our erotic orientation is an aspect of our public identity. There is no getting around it. To welcome us will mean welcoming God's eros in a new way.

Issues such as ordination and the blessing of unions—or, more precisely, the opening of marriage to lesbians and gay men—are not, when all is said and done, about social convenience, or status, or even justice for a minority. It is perfectly legitimate to treat them as a matter of justice; the church has an obligation to behave justly. But they are much more than that. They are about celebrating and acknowledging our eros as one means of our human and Christian communion with God. If lesbians and gay men continue to insist on these matters, it is not merely because we are truculent and uncooperative; it is because they touch on what is central in our relationship with God.

We, of course, already know that our loves give us access to God; we experience it quite directly. We know what Traherne was writing about because we can read it in our own souls and spirits, in our own lives. But the church at large needs to know this, too. And as the church comes to understand it, all Christians will be freed to rediscover the passion of their relatedness to God in new ways. This is not just for lesbians and gay men. It is for everyone.

For those who enjoy the blessing of a life-partner, this is a call to take their love as a grace-filled, joyful opening onto God and to learn how to live in it in ways that honor both the particular, beloved spouse and also the rest of God's beloved world. How can the church help us see the family not simply as a private retreat from the world—and certainly not as the bastion of self-absorption that it keeps threatening to become—but as a center of the spread of God's love? True, the love of the married couple does create a private space, but it is a place where we learn how to be sharers of God's love and are enriched by love to give love.[20]

For those called to celibacy, this is a call to prize passion, not turn away from it—to become more, not less transparent to the intensity of God's love for the world at large. Celibacy as an expectation or demand too often creates narrowness, anger, contempt, hostility, dryness. The celibate person who has received it not as demand but as gift and vocation is unmistakably different. In such persons, celibacy proves its grace-filled possibilities by showing how the eros that most of us attach especially to one particular person can also show itself more broadly.

For those who are single by circumstance, not by vocation, God's eros is a call to see all intimate relationships, sexual or nonsexual, as holy. They are a part of our life in and with God, to be received as reverently and joyfully as God's own self, to be given and received with the consciousness of God's grace offering itself in and through one another. Some of our relationships fail to fulfill the promise of holiness. But we can be honest about this without having to despair of the continuing possibility of grace and blessing.

For the whole church, the rediscovery of eros and of its centrality should refocus our understanding of faith and of the faithful life. Neither can be defined entirely in advance. God calls us, like Abram and Sarai, into the unknown. Before their life with God was completed, they not only moved far from where they were born; they even received new names: Sarah and Abraham. Because our life with God is an erotic journey, we, too, will encounter surprises and experience new things. This is not something to dread, but to welcome. Our home with God, as we begin to see it before us, turns out to be immeasurably more gracious and more beautiful than we could have imagined at the start.

And we ourselves begin to be transformed in ways that begin to fit us for this home, this household. We are transformed by love and for love, learning to love the world alongside the God who made it. Making use of the world without also loving it has brought us to violate the world and

other people with increasingly destructive consequences. As we grasp that our love of God is necessarily worked out in and through our love for
all that God has made, for the world and for the
whole human family, we can begin the work of
rebuilding and repair. The energy for it is love.

Wouldst thou love God alone?
God alone cannot be beloved.

—TRAHERNE

I am the rose of Sharon, and the lily
  of the valleys.
As the lily among thorns, so is my love
  among the daughters.
As the apple tree among the trees of the wood,
  so is my beloved among the sons.
I sat down under his shadow with great delight,
  and his fruit was sweet to my taste.
He brought me to the banqueting house,
  and his banner over me was love.
Stay me with flagons, comfort me with apples:
  for I am sick of love.
His left hand is under my head,
  and his right hand doth embrace me.

—SONG OF SOLOMON 2:1–6 (AV)

ACKNOWLEDGMENTS

$\mathcal{T}$HIS BOOK BEGAN LIFE WHEN I WAS INVITED BY the monks of Glenstal Abbey in Co. Limerick, Ireland, to address their 40th Ecumenical Conference in June 2003. The title of the conference was "Inclining the Ear of the Heart: Voices on Love, Sexuality, and Friendship," and its focus took in a wide range of sexual issues in the contemporary church. I owe a debt of gratitude to the Abbey and to many people with whom I had the pleasure of talking at the conference. If I record a particular debt to Maureen Ryan, Mark Patrick Hederman, and Colm O'Gorman, this is not to imply that my indebtedness stops with them.

By chance, I also lectured at the Atlantic Seminar in Theological Education in Truro, Nova Scotia, in the same month. While I hadn't intended the Glenstal address as part of that conference, it became clear that it belonged there, too. I thank those present for their strong encouragement to continue working with this topic.

In June of 2004, I presented another version of the material to the annual Conference for Rectors of Large Episcopal Churches at the Church Divinity School of the Pacific in Berkeley, California. Several of those attending encouraged me to move toward publication. I am particularly grateful to Jeff Bullock, without whose insistence I might have taken much longer to do so.

Finally, I am grateful to Debra Farrington at Morehouse Publishing, a longtime friend and colleague as well as editor. When I shared with her my perplexities about publication, she was able to suggest a path forward.

The present work, though based on the address for Glenstal Abbey, is not identical to it. Even at the conference, I had to omit some of what I had prepared for reasons of time, and I have taken the opportunity to express other things more fully.

NOTES

THE REASONS FOR THIS BOOK

1. For a powerful statement of this reality, see Mark Patrick Hederman, *Manikon Eros: Mad, Crazy Love* (Dublin: Veritas, 2000).

LOVE HUMAN AND DIVINE

2. *Caritas* and *amor*; three if we include *dilectio*.

3 Interestingly, Augustine, *City of God*, 14.7, specifically rejects this sort of distinction among the Latin terms.

4. E.g., it is absent from the Daily Office lectionary of the first *Book of Common Prayer* (1549) and also that of the present American *Book of Common Prayer* (1979).

5. Marcia Falk, *The Song of Songs: A New Translation* (San Francisco: Harper, 1993; trans. originally published, 1973); Ariel Bloch and Chana Bloch, *The Song of Songs: A New Translation with an Introduction and Commentary* (New York: Random House, 1995).

6. Wilfred Cantwell Smith, *What Is Scripture? A Comparative Approach* (Minneapolis: Fortress, 1993), 21–37.

7. Ann Roberts Winsor, *A King Is Bound in the Tresses: Allusions to the Song of Songs in the Fourth Gospel*, Studies in Biblical Literature, 6 (New York: Peter Lang, 1999).

8. For a pioneering example of such an endeavor, see David M. Carr, *The Erotic Word: Sexuality, Spirituality, and the Bible* (Oxford: Oxford University Press, 2003).

9. Cf. Barbara Hughes Fowler, trans., *Love Lyrics of Ancient Egypt* (Chapel Hill: University of North Carolina Press, 1994); Carr, *Erotic Word*, 91–107.

10. Elizabeth A. Clark, *Ascetic Piety and Women's Faith: Essays on Late Ancient Christianity* (Lewiston, NY: E. Mellen Press, 1986); Peter Brown, *The Body and Society: Men, Women, and Sexual Renunciation in Early Christianity* (New York: Columbia University Press, 1988).

11. Peter Brown, *Augustine of Hippo: A Biography* (Berkeley: University of California Press, 1967), 388–91; cf. *City of God,* 14.16.

12. Thomas Traherne, *Centuries*, introduction by John Farrar (New York: Harper, 1960), 36–37.

13. Aelred of Rievaulx, *Spiritual Friendship,* 1. 57–61.

14. Jean Ponder Soto, "Redeeming Eros: A Christian Ethical Spirituality of Sexual Intimacy" (Ph.D. dissertation, Graduate Theological Union, 2003), drawing on her own interviews with committed Christian couples and also on the work of John M. Gottman and Nan

Silver, *The Seven Principles for Making Marriage Work* (New York: Three Rivers Press, 1999).

15. E.g., Traherne, *Centuries,* 3.1–5.

16. Traherne, *Centuries,* 196.

17. For a penetrating analysis of the importance of the physical in this process, see Rowan Williams, *The Body's Grace,* 10th Michael Harding Memorial Address, 2nd edition (London: Lesbian and Gay Christian Movement, 2002).

18. Thomas Traherne, *Selected Poems and Prose,* ed. Alan Bradford (London: Penguin, 1991), 58–60.

19. Mark Jordan has argued that the repression of sexuality is at least one source of the sexual abuse of the weak in the church: *The Silence of Sodom: Homosexuality in Modern Catholicism* (Chicago: University of Chicago Press, 2000).

20. For an analysis and celebration of this blessing, see Catherine M. Wallace, *For Fidelity: How Intimacy and Commitment Enrich Our Lives* (New York: Vintage Books, 1998).